K

D1407613

THE PORTABLE CRAFTER
BEADING

I shut my eyes
in order to see.
Paul Gaugin

THE PORTABLE CRAFTER
BEADING

Susan Ure

Sterling Publishing Co., Inc.
New York
A Sterling/Chapelle Book

Chapelle, Ltd.
Jo Packham • Sara Toliver • Cindy Stoeckl

Editor: Laura Best
Photography: Ryne Hazen for Hazen Photography
Photo Stylist: Suzy Skadburg
Art Director: Karla Haberstich
Copy Editor: Marilyn Goff
Staff: Kelly Ashkettle, Areta Bingham, Anne Bruns, Donna Chambers,
    Emily Frandsen, Lana Hall, Susan Jorgensen, Jennifer Luman,
    Melissa Maynard, Barbara Milburn, Lecia Monsen, Kim Taylor,
    Linda Venditti, Desirée Wybrow

Library of Congress Cataloging-in-Publication Data

Ure, Susan.
The portable crafter. Beading / Susan Ure.
p. cm.
"A Sterling/Chapelle Book."
Includes index.
ISBN 1-4027-0933-1
1. Beadwork. 2. Jewelry making. I. Title: Beading. II. Title. III.
Portable crafter.
TT860.U74 2004
745.58'2--dc22
2003027781

10 9 8 7 6 5 4 3 2 1

Published by Sterling Publishing Co., Inc.
387 Park Avenue South, New York, NY 10016
©2004 by Susan Ure
Distributed in Canada by Sterling Publishing
c/o Canadian Manda Group, One Atlantic Avenue, Suite 105
Toronto, Ontario, Canada M6K 3E7
Distributed in Great Britain by Chrysalis Books Group PLC
The Chrysalis Building, Bramley Road, London W10 6SP, England
Distributed in Australia by Capricorn Link (Australia) Pty. Ltd.
P.O. Box 704, Windsor, NSW 2756, Australia
Printed in China
All Rights Reserved

Sterling ISBN 1-4027-0933-1

If you have questions or comments, please contact:
    Chapelle, Ltd., Inc.,
    P.O. Box 9252, Ogden, UT 84409
    (801) 621-2777 • (801) 621-2788 Fax
    e-mail: chapelle@chapelleltd.com
    web site: chapelleltd.com

INTRODUCTION

Beading does not require many supplies or much equipment. Wire and beads will suffice for small projects. Beading is a craft that, depending on the size, can be transported easily. This book is filled with projects which can be easily brought along on car trips and airplanes, to soccer games and doctors' offices. Wherever you are found with some extra time, beading will help pass the time.

TABLE OF CONTENTS

BEADING BASICS

Brass—can be quite costly depending on the brass content. There are wide varieties of styles and sizes.

Bugle—are long narrow beads with a center hole running the length of each bead.

Crystal—are glass beads with a diamondlike fire when light-struck. They are made of fine quality glass and are shaped by a mechanized cutting process.

Faceted—are molded glass or plastic beads available with silver or bronze finishes.

Fancy—can vary from cubed, cylindrical, oval, triangular, twisted, and teardrop- and donut-shaped.

Glass—are available in a huge array of sizes, shapes, and colors. They are the most commonly used bead.

Metal—can be costly depending on the precious-metal content. There are wide varieties of styles and sizes of metal beads available in surface-washed base-metal beads.

Seed—are small glass beads, available in a number of finishes and colors.

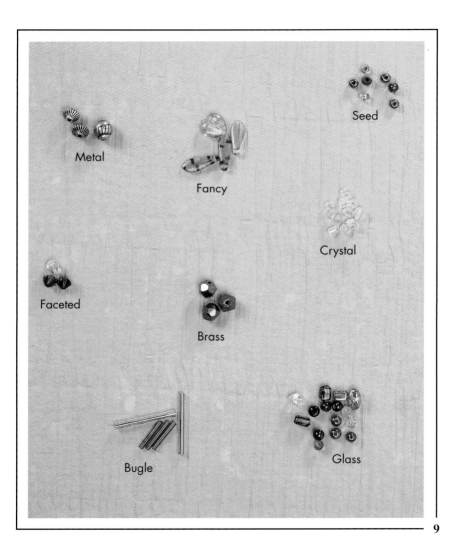

Metal

Fancy

Seed

Crystal

Faceted

Brass

Bugle

Glass

CLASPS

Barrel—is a clasp where the ends screw into one another.

Jump rings—are used to join components. They have a gap in the ring and separate easily with pliers.

Lobster clasps—are used to join close bead strands. They can be used with a jump ring or can be hooked directly to a loop of beads.

Split rings—are like tiny key rings. The ring is doubled onto itself for better surety.

Spring clasp—along with a jump ring makes a two-part metal unit used to close bead strands.

Toggle—is a closure where a bar slips into a ring sideways to secure within the ring.

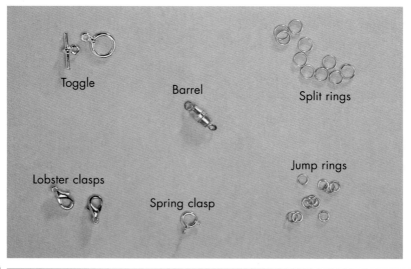

Toggle

Barrel

Split rings

Lobster clasps

Spring clasp

Jump rings

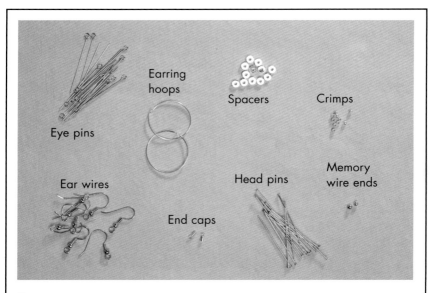

Eye pins

Earring hoops

Spacers

Crimps

Ear wires

Head pins

Memory wire ends

End caps

FINDINGS

Crimps—are small metal tubes that are crushed to hold wires together.

Ear wires—come with loops to hang findings.

Earring hoops—are looped wires worn in the ears.

End caps—cover a final knot, holding strands together.

Eye pins—are wires with a loop on one end.

Head pins—are long rigid wires with one end flattened.

Memory wire ends—are placed on ends of wire to finish off.

Spacers—are used between beads to enhance or fill in spaces.

When selecting wire for your project, choose the heaviest wire that will pass through the smallest hole of your beads.

Bead wire—is soft, supple beading wire made from stainless steel that is coated in nylon. This wire comes in a variety of colors. It is recommended for heavier beads and is available in 7, 19, and 49 strands. Use crimps and a crimp bead to finish ends.

Memory wire—is a flexible coil wire that comes in preformed bracelet, necklace, and ring shapes and accepts a wide variety of bead sizes. This wire is made from hardened steel and requires the use of industrial-strength cutters and pliers.

Metal wire—When selecting a wire size, consider the beads that the wire will be supporting as well as the project use.

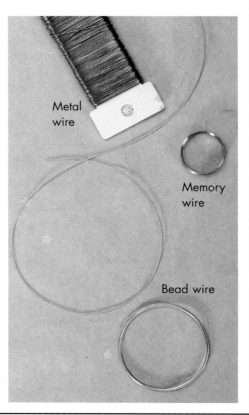

Metal wire

Memory wire

Bead wire

Crimping pliers—are designed especially for crimps. They cinch a smooth crimp without unsightly sharp edges.

Needle-nosed pliers—are used to control wire wrapping, open jump rings, and maintain crimping.

Round-nosed pliers—are used for making loops. Do not use them for gripping to prevent denting soft wire.

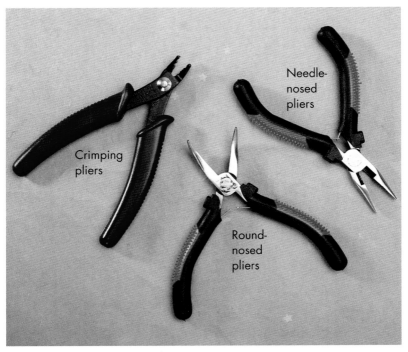

Crimping pliers

Needle-nosed pliers

Round-nosed pliers

13

(right) Use small containers to keep beads sorted and portable.

(below) Keep beads and tools organized and grouped with like items for easy access.

(above) There are numerous products available to assist in keeping your supplies protected and organized.

(above) Leather chamois helps prevent beads from rolling.

(page 17) A beading work board helps keep supplies organized while helping you see a design layout before stringing beads.

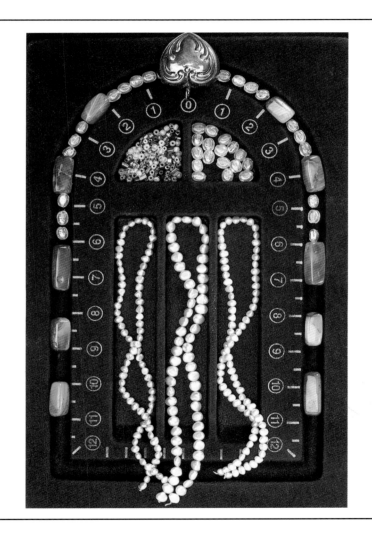

CRYSTAL BRACELET

NEEDED ITEMS
- Beads
    - 8mm crystal bicone (14)
    - 7mm silver disk (5)
    - 3mm silver spacer (2)
- Bead wire, 7 strand (7")
- Masking tape
- Needle-nosed pliers
- Silver toggle
- Wire cutters

INSTRUCTIONS

1. Tape one end of the wire to prevent beads from slipping off.

2. Referring to bead placement in the photograph, slip beads onto wire.

3. Use a spacer on both ends.

4. Using pliers, attach wire ends to toggle.

18

CUBES BRACELET

NEEDED ITEMS

- Beads
  - 5mm glass disk (3)
  - 4mm glass round (6)
  - 4mm glass round (10)
  - 3mm silver spacer (4)
  - 4mm silver square (32)
- Bead wire, 7 strand (7")

- Crimping pliers
- Crimps
- Masking tape
- Needle-nosed pliers
- Silver toggle
- Wire cutters

INSTRUCTIONS

1. Tape one end of wire to prevent beads from slipping off.

2. Referring to bead placement in the photograph, begin in the center and slip beads onto the wire.

3. Run each end of the wire through one crimp, then one ring on the toggle, then back through the crimp. Tie a simple knot.

4. Using pliers, flatten crimps over the knots on both ends.

CORAL BRACELET

NEEDED ITEMS
- Beads
    6mm coral round (7)
    4mm crystal faceted (3)
    4mm glass faceted (3)
    10mm silver rectangle (4)
    4mm silver round (11)
- Bead wire, 7 strand (7")

- Crimping pliers
- Crimps
- Jump ring
- Lobster clasp
- Masking tape
- Wire cutters

INSTRUCTIONS

1. Tape one end of wire to prevent beads from slipping off.

2. Referring to bead placement in the photograph on page 21, slip beads onto wire.

3. Run one wire end through one crimp, ring on the clasp, then back through crimp. Tie a simple knot.

4. Run other wire end through jump ring and back through crimp. Tie a simple knot.

5. Using pliers, flatten crimps over knots on both ends.

6. Thread excess ends of wire back through a few beads on each side.

7. Using wire cutters, trim excess wire close to the bracelet; avoid cutting the bracelet.

STRAND BRACELET

NEEDED ITEMS

- Beads
    - 3mm coral round (18)
    - 4mm glass round (6)
    - 3mm silver disk (6)
    - 3mm silver round (23)
    - 2mm silver round (145)
    - 3mm silver spacer (9)
    - 4mm silver square (13)
- Bead wire, 7 strand (21")
- Masking tape
- Needle-nosed pliers
- Rings
    - 6mm silver (2)
    - 3mm silver (6)
- Silver toggle
- Wire cutters

INSTRUCTIONS

1. Cut wire into thirds.

2. Tape one end of each wire to prevent beads from slipping off.

3. Referring to bead placement in the photograph on page 23, string seventy-eight 2mm silver round beads onto first wire.

4. String beads onto second wire, following the Strand Bracelet Diagram.

STRAND BRACELET DIAGRAM

5. String beads onto the third wire in a random pattern, using five silver 4mm square beads and sixty-seven silver 2mm round beads.

6. Using pliers, attach each strand to a 3mm ring. Attach one ring from each strand to a 6mm ring on both sides. Attach 6mm rings to toggle.

GREEN BRACELET

NEEDED ITEMS

- Beads
  - 8mm brass round (2)
  - 7mm brass round (2)
  - 6mm brass round (1)
  - 4mm brass round (2)
  - 3mm copper bicone (2)
  - 8mm copper disk (2)
  - 5mm copper disk (3)
  - 3mm crystal designer (1)
  - 8mm glass cone (2)
  - 6mm glass dangle (2)
  - 9mm glass decorative (3)
  - 8mm glass disk (2)
  - ¾" glass oblong (1)
  - 6mm glass round (4)
  - 4mm glass round (9)
  - 4mm glass square (3)

- Bead wire, 7 strand (7")
- Brass toggle
- Crimping pliers
- Crimps
- Masking tape
- Needle-nosed pliers
- Wire cutters

INSTRUCTIONS

1. Tape one end of wire to prevent beads from slipping off.

2. Referring to bead placement in the photograph on page 25, string beads onto wire.

3. Run each end of wire through one crimp, one ring on the toggle, then back through crimp. Tie a simple knot.

4. Using pliers, flatten crimps over the knots on both ends.

Note: For the Green Necklace instructions, see pages 54–55.

25

STRETCH MAGIC

NEEDED ITEMS

- Beads
    - 6° glass faceted (4)
    - 8mm glass round (8)
    - #2 metal bugle (8)
    - 12mm metal decorative (3)
    - 8mm metal round (4)
- All-purpose glue
- Elastic thread
- Scissors

INSTRUCTIONS

1. Cut elastic thread approximately 6" longer than desired length of bracelet. The finished strand length should be the wrist measurement plus 1" before tying.

2. Referring to bead placement in the the photograph on page 27, string beads onto thread.

3. Tie thread ends together in a simple knot.

4. Apply dot of glue to knot. Let dry.

5. Trim off excess thread ends.

27

PRIMITIVE BRACELET

NEEDED ITEMS
- Beads
  - 8mm brass disk (1)
  - 7mm brass ring (1)
  - 3mm cork (3)
  - 9mm glass disk (2)
  - 7mm glass drop (2)
  - 16mm glass oblong (2)
  - 9mm glass oval (3)
  - 14mm glass round (3)
  - 9mm glass round (3)
  - 9mm glass square (2)
  - 5mm glass triangle (1)
  - 7mm metal decorative (3)
  - 10mm metal ring (2)
  - 3mm silver spacer (1)

- Bead wire, 7 strand (7")
- Brass toggle
- Crimping pliers
- Crimps
- Masking tape
- Needle-nosed pliers
- Wire cutters

INSTRUCTIONS

1. Tape one end of wire to prevent beads from slipping off.

2. Referring to bead placement in the photograph on page 29, string beads onto wire.

3. Run each end of wire through one crimp, one ring on the toggle, then back through crimp. Tie a simple knot.

4. Using pliers, flatten crimps over the knots on both ends.

INDIAN BRACELET

NEEDED ITEMS

- Beads
  - assorted glass (10)
  - assorted metal (3)
  - assorted seed (20)
- Bead wire, 7 strand (10")
- Crimping pliers

- Crimps
- Decorative Indian button
- Masking tape
- Needle-nosed pliers
- Wire cutters

INSTRUCTIONS

1. Tape one end of wire to prevent beads from slipping off.

2. Referring to bead placement in the photograph on page 31, slip beads on wire to 7" length.

3. Run one end of wire through one crimp and through the Indian head button, back through the crimp. Using pliers, flatten the crimp. Leave a very small amount of slack in wire (no more than ½") when attaching clasp to prevent bracelet from being too rigid.

4. Thread excess ends of wire back through a few beads on each side and trim close to necklace, taking care to avoid cutting bracelet.

5. On the loop end, slip on one crimp and 2" of small glass beads. Thread the wire back through the crimp and pull tight. Using pliers, flatten crimps. Be certain the loop is large enough to fit the button through comfortably.

CUFF BRACELET

NEEDED ITEMS
- Beads
    - 6°–11° assorted beads
- Block of wood
- Round-nosed pliers
- Small hammer
- Wire cutters
- Wires
    - 18-gauge (6')
    - 26-gauge (1 spool)

Designed by Mary Lowe

INSTRUCTIONS

1. Fold the 18-gauge wire in half and twist together 6" from the fold. Shape wire into a 1"x6" oval. (A)

A

2. Weave one tail back and forth, around and across the 1" span. At the end, loop the wire around twice and weave back, occasionally wrap the wire over twice to strengthen the design. Using pliers, curl up the last inch. Repeat with the other tail. (B)

B

C

3. Place flat cuff on wood and hammer lightly on one side. It will naturally curl up, and harden the wire. Using fingers, shape cuff until desired shape.

4. Using 2' of the 26-gauge wire and pliers, coil the last inch. String a flower up to the coil and wrap the wire around the 18-gauge frame. (C)

5. String beads to reach another wire junction and wrap the beaded wire around the base wire. Continue adding beads to the cuff and end the wire with another flower curl.

6. Repeat with more wires until you are satisfied with the density of the beads.

TWISTED CAB

NEEDED ITEMS
- Beads
  - 6° seed (20g)
  - 11° seed (21g)
- Labradorite cab
- Needle
- Split ring (2)
- Thread
- Toggle

Designed by Doris Coghill

INSTRUCTIONS
Triangular base (using 6° seeds)

1. Brick stitch is traditionally started with a row of beads, ladder-stitched together. Following is an alternative method that is easier to hold onto and keeps a more even tension.

2. Using doubled thread, pick up three beads. Go through bead farthest from the needle. (A)

3. Pull beads together; you will end up with a "T" shape. (B) They should not look like C.

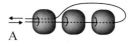

A

B

C

4. Pick up a bead and go through the top part of the "T". It will start to look like a two-row peyote stitch. Continue in the same manner, picking up one bead and going through the lower bead.

5. Thread should be coming out of the top of the last bead of the previous row. Pick up two beads and push the needle under the second thread, then back up the second bead (should be directly above the thread.) (D)

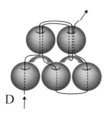

D ↑

6. Go down through the first bead of the new row and the second bead of the previous row, then up the third bead in the previous row and the second bead in the new row.

Continue with regular brick stitch for the rest of the row.

7. Complete one center section and two of the end sections with brick stitch. (E) You will be starting each piece at its widest part and working a decreasing brick stitch. For the center section, start in the center, with one bead in the widest row, and work to one end. Weave the thread back to the center and complete the other side.

Attaching clasps

8. When you have completed the end piece, your thread should be coming out of one of the two end beads. Pick up six of 11° seed beads and the split ring. Form a loop by going down the other bead of the end row. For strength, weave the thread down one more row and then back up and go through the loop of six seed beads again. Weave the thread down a few rows. Tie a knot;

weave the thread through a few more beads. If you have a short thread, you can cut it off at this point. If you have a longer thread, you can use it to do the twist part and attach it to the center of the bracelet. Repeat for the other end of the bracelet.

Determining bracelet size

9. After all the brick-stitched pieces are complete and the clasp is attached, lay the piece out to determine the length of the bracelet. The length of the twist between the brick-stitched pieces can be adjusted to make the bracelet larger or smaller. The twisting part between the brick-stitched pieces will shorten the length of the bracelet. Be certain to take this into consideration when calculating the length of the seed-bead strands that will make up the twist.

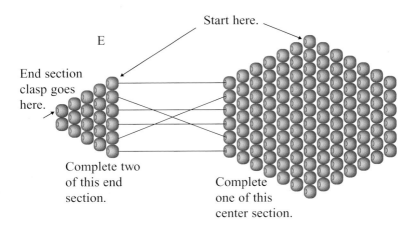

Start here.

E

End section clasp goes here.

Complete two of this end section.

Complete one of this center section.

Twist

10. The twist between the brick-stitched pieces is done using thirty to thirty-five 11° seed beads. The amount will depend on the bracelet size.

11. The lines in (E) on page 37, represent coming out of a bead in one brick-stitched section and going directly into the corresponding bead in the other brick-stitched section. Do one or two strands on each side, then check to be certain that you have figured the length of the bracelet accurately. The twists will shorten the bracelet.

12. To complete the first twist, hold bracelet with clasp away from you. Divide four strands in half. Bring clasp end down through the separation and back away from you. Repeat. Manipulate the strands until they are lying evenly.

13. Using 11° seed beads, complete the first of the red lines. For the second red line, string on enough seed beads to reach to the bead on the other side. Before going into the bead on the other side, wrap the strand of seed beads around the first strand once. Complete another set of twists on the other side.

Adding cab

14. Position the cab on the center brick-stitched section so one bead shows in the top and bottom of the cab. *Note: You may want to put a small spot of glue in the center back of the cab to hold in place while creating the bezel. Let the bracelet sit for at least 30 minutes to dry.*

15. Using a single thread, weave through several rows of the brick stitch. Anchor thread with a knot and weave through several more of the brick-stitched beads. Come out at the edge of the cab.

16. Do a "backstitch" of color 2, 11° seed beads around the cab. (F) Come up through the base. Pick up four color 2 seed beads. Lay them along the side of the cab and put the needle down through the base at the end of the fourth bead. Come back up through the base between the second and third bead and go through the third and fourth bead. Repeat around the cab. Go through the center of the beads in the base or around thread between beads to get the line of 11° as close to the edge of the cab as possible. Thread should not show on the back of the bracelet.

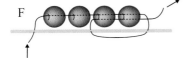

17. Continue around the cab with two rows of peyote-stitch, using color 2 of the 11° beads. The final row of the bezel will be the 14° seed beads color 3. After the last row is complete, run the needle and thread (without) around the same thread path to strengthen the bezel. Weave your needle through to the bottom of the bezel and use the same thread for the bezel accent row.

Accent around the bezel

18. After finishing the bezel, weave thread down to the base row of the bezel and come out of any of the beads in that row. Pick up one color 2 11° seed bead (the same color as the bezel.) Skip a bead and go through the next bead in the bottom row. What you are doing is a peyote-stitched row that is attached to the bottom row of the bezel and will lie on the brick-stitched base.

NETTED BRACELET

NEEDED ITEMS
- Beads
    - 11° seed white (10 g)
    - 11° seed gold (10 g)
    - 4mm–6mm gold (24–30)
- Lobster clasp
- Needle, size 10
- Scissors
- Split rings
- Thread

Designed by Doris Coghill

INSTRUCTIONS

Note: These directions make a 7"–8" bracelet. For a longer one, add more rows to each side.

Basic Netting:

1. Thread needle with two yards of thread. Leave a 15" tail to add the clasp.

2. String on three white, one gold, three white, one gold, three white, and one gold seed beads.

3. Form a ring with the beads and tie a square knot. Pass the needle through the gold bead, next to the knot.

4. String on two white seed, one gold seed, two white seed, and go through the next gold bead in the ring. Repeat two more times. (A)

A

Point beads

5. Continue through two white seed and one gold seed beads (in the first row—not the original ring.) Thread should now be coming out of a gold bead (or point bead.) This will set you up for the first stitch of the next row.

6. Repeat Steps 4 and 5 on page 40 until you have approximately 1". Tie a square knot and weave thread back toward the start of the netted tube for 1". Cut off thread.

7. Lay this piece aside and make another one just like it, except this time use three yards of thread. Do not tie off the thread on the second piece.

Center Twist

8. Lay both netted pieces on a surface facing each other. The last one completed should have a thread coming out of a point bead. Be certain you have the netted ends facing and not the beginning ends. The netted end will have a pattern of two white seed, one gold seed, and two white seed beads. The beginning ends will have a pattern of three white, one gold, and three white seed beads.

9. Lay out your selection of accent beads, dividing them into eight sections with three to six beads in each section. Divide the largest beads evenly among the sections. The accent beads should be 4mm–6mm.

10. Pick up a combination of gold seed beads and one of the eight sections of accent beads. This bead combination should measure 1½".

11. Go through two beads on the end row of the other piece of netting. Repeat Steps 10 and 11 three more times, continuing around the circle.

12. After picking up the next group of 1½" go through three beads instead of two. Continue with three more rows going through two beads. You should have a total of eight rows of 1½" spaced evenly around the circle of netting.

13. Tie a square knot and weave thread into the netting approximately 2". Cut thread. (B)

14. To complete the "twist", divide the eight strands in half. Bring the clasp end of the netted tube closest to you down through this separation and back toward you. This will form the twist of 1½" lengths.

15. Manipulate strands until they are laying evenly. If the twist seems lopsided because of more large beads on one side than the other, simply untwist it, divide the strands so that the largest beads appear evenly spaced, and then retwist.

Attach Clasp

16. Place needle on a 15" piece of thread attached to the beginning of the netted tube. Thread should be coming out of the center white seed bead in a group of three seed beads.

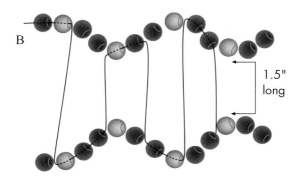

B

1.5" long

17. Pick up one white seed, one gold seed, one white seed, and go through the center white seed bead in the next group of three white seed beads. Repeat twice. On the final stitch, continue through one white seed and one gold seed beads. Thread should be coming out of the point gold seed bead. (C)

18. Pick up one gold seed bead and go through the next gold seed in the circle. Continue around and join the circle.

Pick up six gold seed beads and a split ring or one side of the clasp and pass through the gold seed bead on the opposite side of the circle. Reinforce by going halfway around the circle and back through the loop holding the clasp as many times as the beads will allow.

19. Tie off thread and weave end back into the netting for approximately 2". Cut off thread. Repeat for other half of the clasp.

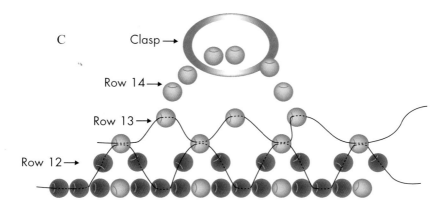

C   Clasp →

Row 14→

Row 13→

Row 12→

BEADED WATCH

NEEDED ITEMS
- Beads
    6mm cubes (40–50)
    assorted seed
- Beading work board
- Needle, size 10
- Scissors

- Thread
- Toggle
- Watch face with removable
    bar attachments

Designed by Linda Gettings

INSTRUCTIONS

1. Remove bar attachment from watch and set aside. Using a single strand of thread 2'–3' long, attach a waste bead, leaving at least a 6" tail to weave into your piece later.

2. Pick up two cube beads and slide them to touch the waste bead. Move the second cube to sit next to the first cube and weave them together by taking the needle and thread up through the bottom of the first cube and down through the top of the second cube. Repeat two more times. *Note: Add thread by tying on a new one, using a knot you feel comfortable with. A dab of glue will keep it from slipping.*

3. Continue adding one cube at a time in this same manner until you have completed half of the watch strap. Repeat to finish the other half of strap. *Note: To get a tight fit on your*

45

*wrist, run a ribbon around
your wrist and cut it at a
comfortable length. Divide
this length in half, then
subtract the length of the
watch face. Or set the watch
face in the middle of the
ribbon and check the length
as you weave.*

4. Attach the bands to the watch
    face by sliding the bar through
    the last cube bead on each
    strap half. Pop the bars back
    into place on the watch.

5. Attach toggle ends by weaving
    ends together. Be certain to
    weave back and forth through
    the cube and toggle attach-
    ment at least three or four
    more times to secure.

6. To embellish, take the needle
    and doubled thread through
    the first cube and pick up the
    desired number of beads in
    the desired order. *Note: To add
    stability to embellishments,*

*run a slip knot between the
cubes, using the threads
that connect the cubes to
each other.*

7. Begin with one or two 13°
    seed beads to make each
    embellishment more flexible
    and loose hanging. Then add
    one or two random beads
    followed by one 11° seed as
    the anchor.

8. To anchor your line of beads,
    take the needle and thread
    around the last 13° seed bead
    and back up through the beads
    in your row and out through
    the other side of the cube.

9. Repeat, moving down to the
    watch bar. Pick up a few 11°
    seed beads and take needle
    and thread over and around
    the bar on both sides of the
    cube holding it in place.
    Embellish the piece as little
    or as much as desired. Repeat
    for second side.

BRASS BRACELET

- Beads
    - ½" brass bugle (2)
    - ¾" brass finial (1)
    - 4mm brass oval (1)
    - 3mm brass ring (4)
    - 3mm crystal faceted (5)
    - 3mm crystal oblong (3)
    - 5mm pearl seed (3)
- Bead wire, 7 strand (7")
- Brass toggle
- Crimping pliers
- Crimps
- Masking tape
- Needle-nosed pliers
- Wire cutters

INSTRUCTIONS

1. Tape one end of wire to prevent beads from slipping off.

2. Begin with 1" oblong brass in the middle and work out to ends. Referring to bead placement in the photograph, string beads onto wire.

3. Run each end of wire through one crimp, one ring on the toggle, then back through crimp. Tie a simple knot.

4. Using pliers, flatten crimps over the knots on both ends.

Note: For Brass Necklace instructions, see pages 49–51.

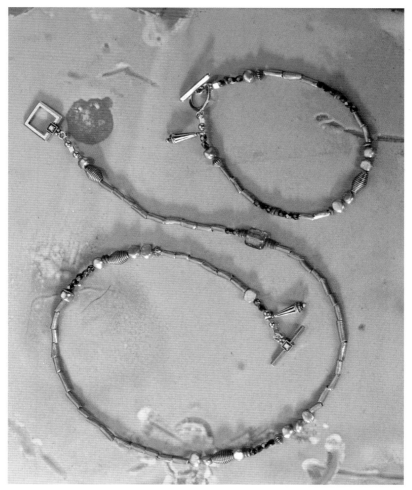

BRASS NECKLACE

NEEDED ITEMS

- Beads
  ½" brass bugle (10)
  1" brass finial (1)
  1" brass oblong (1)
  ¾" brass oblong (1)
  3mm brass ring (7)
  3mm crystal faceted (18)
  9mm glass square (1)
  gold round (2)
  ½" gold bicone (3)
  5mm pearl seed (6)

- Bead wire, 7 strand (22")
- Brass square toggle
- Crimping pliers
- Crimps
- Masking tape
- Needle-nosed pliers
- Wire cutters

INSTRUCTIONS

1. Tape one end of wire to prevent beads from slipping off.

2. Referring to bead placement in the photograph on page 51, string beads onto wire.

3. Run each end of wire through one crimp, one ring on the toggle, then back through crimp. Tie a simple knot.

4. Using pliers, flatten crimps over the knots on both ends.

Note: For Brass Bracelet instructions, see pages 48–49.

Project 15

BONE NECKLACE

NEEDED ITEMS

- Beads
  - 1" bone oblong (4)
  - 8° cork seed (24)
  - 6mm glass disk (4)
  - 5mm x 7mm glass oval (4)
  - 16mm glass round (1)
  - 12mm glass round (2)
  - 4mm glass round (19)
  - 4mm assorted (13)
- Bead wire, 7 strand (20")
- Crimping pliers
- Crimps
- Gold clasp
- Masking tape
- Needle-nosed pliers
- Wire cutters

INSTRUCTIONS

1. Tape one end of wire to prevent beads from slipping off.
2. String center bead onto wire, then work out from center on both sides to the ends matching your design on both sides.
3. Referring to the photograph on page 53, string beads onto wire.
4. Using pliers, attach end of wire to clasp.

I shut my eyes
in order to see.
Paul Gauguin

GREEN NECKLACE

NEEDED ITEMS
- Beads
    - 8mm brass disks (7)
    - 3mm brass rings (20)
    - 6mm glass dangle (1)
    - 9mm glass decorative (1)
    - 6mm glass decorative (6)
    - 8mm glass disk (1)
    - ¾" glass oblong (17)
    - 4mm glass round (41)

- Bead wire, 7 strand (23")
- Brass clasp
- Crimping pliers
- Crimps
- Masking tape
- Needle-nosed pliers
- Wire cutters

INSTRUCTIONS

1. Tape one end of wire to prevent beads from slipping off.

2. Referring to bead placement in the photograph on page 55, string beads onto wire. *Note: You may choose to use a different random style. Such a design requires a balance in the visual and actual weight of the beads.*

3. Run each end of wire through one crimp, one ring on the clasp, then back through crimp. Tie a simple knot.

4. Using pliers, flatten crimps over the knots on both ends.

Note: For Green Bracelet instructions, see pages 24–25.

PROJECT 17

PEARL NECKLACE

NEEDED ITEMS

- Beads
    - 25mm abalone oblong (4)
    - 8mm abalone round (3)
    - 8mm crystal bicone (16)
    - 7mm silver disk (9)
    - 15° silver seed (14)
- Beading cord
- End cap (2)

- Lobster clasp
- Masking tape
- Needle
- Needle-nosed pliers
- Scissors
- Tape measure
- Thin drinking straw

INSTRUCTIONS

1. Tape one end of wire to prevent beads from slipping off.

2. Use the largest cord that your beads will accommodate. Measure twice the finished length of your necklace.

3. Cut straw to use as a spacer between knots. Slice the straw on the side and it will slip on and off with ease.

4. Referring to bead placement in the photograph on page 57, string beads onto cord. After each bead that you desire a space, make a single overhand knot against the bead tip. Wrap the end of this cord around the four fingers of your left hand, drop the bead tip into the loop of the knot with your right hand. Placing needle in the knot for better control will be helpful.

5. Tie knot and attach an end cap to each cord. Using pliers, attach end caps to clasp.

HEART PENDANT

NEEDED ITEMS

- Beads
  - 6mm glass bicone (100)
  - 3mm silver spacer (1)
- Bead wire, 7 strand (22")
- Crimping pliers
- Crimps
- Head pin

- Heart pendant
- Jump ring
- Lobster clasp
- Masking tape
- Needle-nosed pliers
- Silver chain (2")
- Wire cutters

INSTRUCTIONS

1. Tape one end of wire to prevent beads from slipping off.

2. Referring to bead placement in the photograph on page 59, slip pendant onto wire center. String beads on both sides of pendant to 16" length.

3. Run each end of wire through one crimp, one ring on clasp, and back through the crimp. Using pliers, flatten crimps. *Note: Leave some slack in bead wire (no more than ⅛")* *when attaching clasp to prevent necklace from being too rigid.* Thread excess ends of wire back through a few beads on each side and trim close to necklace, avoid cutting necklace.

4. Attach jump ring to chain. Slide spacer and a bead onto the head pin. Using pliers, make circle. Slip it through the jump ring and wrap around the rest of the head pin to complete the circle.

BEAD DROPS

NEEDED ITEMS

- Beads
    - 8mm metal decorative (2)
    - 6mm metal disks (2)
    - 10mm turquoise oval (1)
    - 8mm turquoise round (2)
    - 6mm turquoise square (2)
- Ear wires (2)

- Indian-head button
- Lobster clasp
- Round-nosed pliers
- Silver head pins (3)
- Suede cord (20")
- Wire cutters

Designed by Kim Edwards

INSTRUCTIONS

1. Tie a knot in one end of cord. Referring to bead placement in the photograph on page 61, slip beads on head pins. Using wire cutters, trim each head pin to ⅜" beyond last bead.

2. Using pliers, form a loop in end of head pin. Slip loop on ear wire loop and close.

3. Thread button onto cord, followed by three earring drops and back through button.

4. Slip clasp onto one end of suede and secure with a knot. Tie looped knot in other end for clasp to hook to.

DROP EARRINGS

NEEDED ITEMS
- Beads
  - 6° seed (10)
  - 6mm silver disks (2)
- Ear wires (2)

- Round-nosed pliers
- Silver head pins (10)
- Wire cutters

Designed by Kim Edwards
INSTRUCTIONS

1. Referring to photograph, slip beads on head pins.

2. Using wire cutters, trim each head pin to ⅜" beyond last bead.

3. Using pliers, form a loop in end of head pin. Slip loop on ear wire and close.

4. Make five drops for each ear wire and close.

LOOP EARRINGS

NEEDED ITEMS
- Beads
    - 10x14mm glass round (2)
    - 10mm glass faceted (2)
    - 6mm silver spacers (2)
- Ear wire loops (2)
- Round-nosed pliers
- Silver head pins (2)
- Wire cutters

Designed by Kim Edwards

INSTRUCTIONS

1. Referring to the photograph, slip beads and spacers onto head pins.

2. Using wire cutters, trim each head pin to ⅜" beyond last bead.

3. Using pliers, form a loop in end of head pin. Slip loop on ear wire and close.

BEADED HEADBAND

NEEDED ITEMS

- Beads
  - 4mm glass round (6)
  - 3mm glass round (6)
- Glass flowers
  - large (1)
  - small (2)

- Wire cutters
- Wires
  - 16-gauge copper
  - 16-gauge silver

INSTRUCTIONS

1. Using silver and copper wires, bend into shape to fit head—approximately 12". Twist copper wire around the silver to form headband.

2. Cut 8" lengths of silver wire. Attach glass floret with 4mm beads wired in the center of the small flowers and 3mm beads in large flower.

3. Twist silver wire and the ends of wires from the flowers together. Take remaining silver wire and twist together. Wrap around headband.

4. Wrap another silver wire around top portion of headband, coiling ends for design.

GRAPE LOOP

NEEDED ITEMS

- Beads
  - 6mm glass disk (7)
  - 3mm glass round (30)
- Glass grape charm

- Jump ring
- Memory wire, 1 coil (6")
- Needle-nosed pliers

Designed by Ester Ure

INSTRUCTIONS

1. Using pliers, bend one end of memory wire into a loop.

2. Strand beads in a five 3mm, one 6mm pattern around wire until you have approximately ¼"–½" left at end of wire.

3. Bend remaining wire and connect. Loop jump ring into the stem of the grape charm and dangle from the center of the ring.

HOT PEPPER LOOP

NEEDED ITEMS
- Beads
    - 6mm glass disk (8)
    - 8mm glass round (3)
    - 6mm glass round (8)
- Chili pepper charms (2)
- Jump ring
- Memory wire, 1 coil (6")
- Needle-nosed pliers

Designed by Ester Ure

INSTRUCTIONS

1. Using pliers, bend one end of memory wire into a loop.

2. Strand beads randomly around wire until you have approximately ¼"–½" left at end of wire.

3. Bend remaining end of wire and connect. Loop jump ring into the loops at the top of glass chili pepper charms and dangle from the center of the ring.

BEADED GIRL

NEEDED ITEMS
- Beads
    - 1½" glass bugle (2)
    - ½" glass bugle (2)
    - 6mm x 8mm glass oval (2)
    - 16mm glass round (1)
    - 6mm glass round (2)
    - 6° seed (6)
- Buttons (2)
- Feather
- Needle-nosed pliers
- Silver wire, 16-gauge
- Wire cutters

Designed by Connie Casto

INSTRUCTIONS

1. Cut 8" piece from wire. Run wire through 1½" bugle, 6x8mm round and back up through bugle. Run through button, then repeat through remaining bugle and round beads. Twist the wire ends together, forming legs.

2. Cut 3½" from wire. String three seeds, one oval, two ½" bugle, one oval, and three seeds. Using pliers, curl the ends to hold beads in place, forming hands.

3. Cut 4" from wire. String "head" button in center. String both ends through "body" bead, then through "body" button. Using pliers, twist wires together to secure.

4. Cut 3" piece from wire. String through "head" button. Slip feather into "head" button. Wrap wire around feather quill, then center of arms to secure in place. Twist wires around body.

BEADED SOLDIER

NEEDED ITEMS
- Beads
    - 1" glass bugle (2) (legs)
    - 8mm glass decorative (2)
    - ¼" glass rectangle (2)
    - 12mm glass round (1) (head)
    - 8mm glass round (2)
    - ½" metal decorative (2)
    - 6° seeds (10)
- Buttons, ¾" decorative (2)
- Feather
- Floral tape
- Needle-nosed pliers
- Silver wire, 16-gauge
- Wire cutters

Designed by Connie Casto

INSTRUCTIONS

1. Cut 8" piece from wire. String through 1" bugle, one seed, one rectangle, and back up through bugle. String through "body" button, then repeat for remaining leg. Twist wire ends together.

2. Cut 3½" from wire. String three seed beads, one 8mm round, one ½" metal, one 8mm decorative, and one seed bead. Run wire back through beads. Repeat for remaining arm.

3. Wrap floral tape around bottom of feather. Slip feather quill through decorative metal button. Run wire through 12mm round, then around feather.

4. Cut 4" piece from wire. String "head" button in center. String both ends through "body" bead, then through "body" button. Using pliers, twist wires together.

70

BEADED MASK

NEEDED ITEMS
- Beads
  - 4mm glass assorted (100)
  - 15mm glass faceted (12)
  - 8mm glass faceted (100)
  - 4mm glass oval (50)
- Beading wire
- Crimps, 2mm
- Feathers (2 pkgs.)
- Glitter
- Hot-glue gun & glue sticks
- Plastic mask
- Ribbon (1')
- Wire cutters
- Wooden dowel (12")

INSTRUCTIONS

1. Layer feathers small to large, filling in empty spaces. Glue feathers to back side of mask.

2. Adhere 8mm beads in a line over nose bridge, slowly working from center to side and tip, filling in empty spaces. Let dry thoroughly.

3. Adhere 15mm beads to top of mask and hide the seam between edge and feathers. Leave spaces for smaller beads. Using 4mm oval beads, fill in space between 15mm beads and layer on top of mask.

4. Wrap dowel in ribbon, gluing at top and bottom. Glue to inside corner of mask.

5. Making a loop with the beading wire, use a crimp to fasten down. Randomly string colored crystal cut beads approximately 6"–7" down and using crimps fasten to secure. Make second string approximately 8"–10" and crimp at bottom to secure. Hot-glue top loop of wires to mask back.

SPIDER WEB

- Beads
  - 11° glass round, clear (64)
  - 4° glass round, clear (21)
  - 6° glass round, gray (150)
  - 15mm designer (2)
- All-purpose glue
- Silver twist wire
- Wire cutters

INSTRUCTIONS

Web

1. Using wire cutters, cut four 8"-long center wires. Slide wires through 4° clear bead. Dot glue to secure wires.

2. On every other center wire, string four to six beads. Twist wire at bottom of bead to secure. Approximately 2½" out from center, weave a piece of wire in a circular direction, twisting center wires around to hold in place.

3. Weave another circular string of clear beads on the opposite center wires 3" from the last circular wire. Use six to eight beads per wire. Twist center wire around this circular wire.

4. Attach another wire circle to center wires approximately 2½" out. Stagger clear beads to match the first set of beads.

5. Twist center wire around outer circle, leaving end wires to dangle.

Spider

6. String fifteen to twenty gray beads onto seven cut wires. Wrap remaining wire ends around web to secure each leg onto web.

7. String designer beads onto center of 2" length of wire. Run wire ends through one to two seed beads, then string through one designer bead.

Wrap wire ends around one another to secure body. Wrap additional wire around body center to secure body onto legs.

BEADED BASKET

NEEDED ITEMS

- Beads
  11° glass, plastic, and wooden round
- Flat-nosed pliers
- Round-nosed pliers

- Metal-ribbed basket
- Wire, 26- or 28-gauge, in a color to complement your bead choices
- Wire cutters

Designed by Denise Perreault

INSTRUCTIONS

1. Cut a manageably long length of wire. Using flat-nosed pliers, wrap wire a few times around a rib near the bottom of the basket, leaving a 1" tail.

2. Twist tail around working wire and bend it around rib to hide and secure it.

3. Use working wire to string enough beads to fill the space between the first two ribs.

4. Wrap beaded wire over and around second rib to create a stack of two wires, one above the other, on the outside of each rib.

5. Continue to string enough beads to snugly fill each section between ribs.

6. Just before wrapping each new section around a rib, give the beaded wire a tug to settle beads onto the wire and make a straight, flat finish for each section.

The above basket is 10½" high x 37" diameter. If you cannot find a basket these exact dimensions the concept is the same for other found basket frames and other wire structures. Just adjust the size and amount of beads used.

7. String beads between ribs separately to ensure that the design will be accurate and to compensate for less-than-symmetrical spacing on the basket form. Also, time won't be wasted trying to keep the beads from sliding off the wire while working.

8. Continue stringing beads and wrapping the wire around each vertical rib until you have completed one row.

9. If you are using seed beads, as in the pyramid patterns at the top and bottom of the basket shown on page 77, wrap the first rib of the second row just above, or below, depending on where you began, and continue stringing beads and wrapping the wire around successive ribs.

10. If you are using larger beads, like the ones at the center of this basket, it will require a second wrap around the first rib of the next row to compensate for the extra width between rows.

11. To add a new wire, wrap the old wire around its vertical rib twice and leave a 1" tail. Twist the tail together with the beginning of a new wire and wrap the twisted tail around the rib to hide it.

12. To replace missing wooden handles, string wooden beads onto a length of aluminum tubing and crimp the tubing onto the handle supports.

13. To wrap the handles and the top rim, string seed beads onto a yard of wire and wrap these portions until they are covered. You may choose to leave space between wraps, or wrap the wire close together to completely cover the steel beneath.

CARD HOLDER

NEEDED ITEMS
- Beads
    - 2mm glass oval (2)
    - 3mm glass round (2)
    - 1mm glass round (4)
- Business card
- Copper wire (12")
- Flat-nosed pliers
- Needle-nosed pliers

Designed by Kim Edwards

INSTRUCTIONS

1. Using a business card as a size guide, find center of the wire. Using pliers, bend a 3" section to form front middle of "chair". Bend small dips at each end for leg.

2. String 3mm bead at each dip. Bend sides backward and bend the same small dips into place for back legs.

3. Crisscross ends of wire across one another at back center, then up across top. Twist wire into spirals attaching 2mm beads and 1mm beads to finish top spirals.

BEADED DRAGONFLY

NEEDED ITEMS
- Beads
    - 8mm glass faceted (1)
    - 4mm glass faceted (30)
    - 9° glass 3-cuts (3 strands)
- Wire cutters

- Wires
    - 24-gauge artistic (wings)
    - 28- or 29-gauge artistic
    - 30-gauge artistic (lacing)

Designed by Donna DeAngelis Dickt

INSTRUCTIONS
Body and head

1. String five 9° beads onto 12" piece of 28- or 29-gauge wire and hold them approximately 3" from one end of the wire. Take the 3" end of the wire and pass it back through beads skipping the first bead. (A)

2. Pull the wire through and push the beads so they are tight up against the first bead and do not move. (B)

3. Using wire cutters, cut short wire close to the beads. (C)

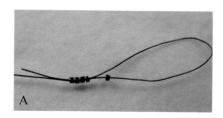

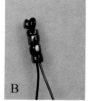

4. To form the body and tail, add enough beads to the other end of the wire until you have 3" of beads on the wire.

5. Add 8mm bead followed by a seed bead to the wire, holding the 8mm bead so there are no spaces between it and the 3" of seed beads. Pass the wire back through the 8mm and pull tightly until all beads are as tight as possible. (D)

6. Add 1½" of beads to the wire. Twist the two strands together until you run out of the 1½" of beads. (E)

7. Wrap bare wire between two beads on the tail four or five times to secure. Cut wire close to the wraps. (F)

Wings

8. On 24-gauge wire, string 22" of 9° beads randomly mixed with thirty 4mm faceted beads. For example, start with ½" of seed beads and add a 4mm bead, then add 1" of seed beads and a 4mm bead. Follow this with ¾" of seed beads and another 4mm bead, and so on until all 22" are strung. *Note: Leave the beads on the spool.*

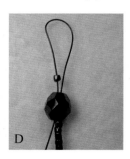

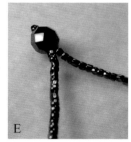

Large wing (make two)

9. Make a double loop with the first loop containing 2½" of beads. Leave a 3" tail at the beginning of the loop. The double loop should have a little space between the loops.

10. Twist spool wire and tail wire for approximately 1" and cut wire from the spool. Repeat for the second wing.

11. Place the two wings face-to-face and twist the stem wires at the base of the wings for 1". Open the wings flat.

Small wing (make two)

12. Make a double loop with the first loop containing 1¾" of beads. Leave a 3" tail at the beginning of the loop. The double loop should have a little space between the loops.

13. Twist spool wire and tail wire for approximately 1" and cut from the spool wire. Repeat for second wing.

14. Place the two wings face-to-face and twist the stem wires at the base of the wings for 1". Open the wings flat.

15. Place the smaller wings on top of the larger wings at approximately the center of the larger wings so they overlap. Use 30-gauge wire to wrap the two stems together for ½" to secure.

16. Using wire cutters, cut wings' stems to a length of ¾". (G)

G

Assembly

17. String 12" of seed beads onto 28- or 29-gauge wire.

18. Beginning just beneath the 8mm bead, wrap the beads around the body six times. (H)

19. Place the body on top of the wings and secure with 30-gauge wire. Continue to wrap the beads around the body, being certain to cover the stems of the wings. Stop wrapping when the body is no longer twisted and the tail begins. (I)

20. Push away any excess beads. Wrap bare wire from the same strand between two beads on the tail. Wrap five times to secure, then cut very close to the body. Take a piece of 30-gauge wire and secure upper body to wings just beneath the head, if necessary. (J)

I

H

J

BOOKMARK

NEEDED ITEMS

- Beads
  - 3mm glass round (2)
  - 2mm glass round (4)

- Needle-nosed pliers
- Wire, 14-gauge (24")
- Wire cutters

Designed by Kim Edwards

INSTRUCTIONS

1. Using pliers, twist wire into desired size coil (approximately 2") with 2mm bead in the center.

2. Begin twisting wire in a free-form style, adding beads as you go.

3. Continue zigzagging wire, twisting into another coil at opposite end.

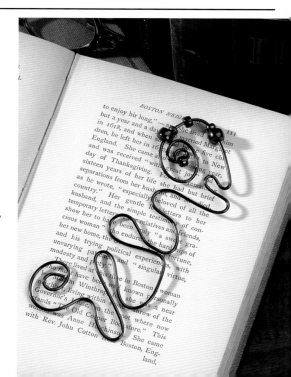

BEADED FLOWER

NEEDED ITEMS
- Beads
  - 14° seed center color
    - (4 strands)
  - 14° seed leaf color
    - (4 strands)
  - 14° seed petal color (1 hank)
- Bead spinner
- Floral tape matching leaf
- Nylon pliers
- Ruler

- Wire cutters
- Wires
  - 30-gauge artistic, (leaf color)
  - 28-gauge artistic, (assembly)
  - 26-gauge artistic,
    - (center color)
  - 26-gauge artistic, (leaf color)
  - 26-gauge, artistic,
    - (petal color)
  - 18-gauge, stem wire

Designed by Donna DeAngelis Dickt

INSTRUCTIONS

Three-loop center (make one)

1. String one strand of center beads onto center wire. Make three continuous loops with seven center-colored beads in each loop. Leave a 3" tail at the beginning and the end. (A)

A

2. Press the three loops together and twist the two tail wires together to form one stem wire. (B)

B

Five-loop center (make one)

3. Make five continuous loops with seven center-colored beads in each loop. Leave 3" tail at beginning and end. (C)

4. Form a circle with the five loops. Twist two tail wires together to form one stem wire. (D)

5. Insert the three loops into the center of the five loops. Cup the five loops around the three loops. Twist the two stem wires together to form one stem wire. (E) Set aside until assembly.

Stamens (make one)

6. Make last part of center by forming a loop with one bead on the wire. Make loop no more than ¼" high. Leave a 3" tail at the beginning.

7. Twist loop wire together until the bead sits at stem top. (F)

8. Make the next loop of wire,

C

D

E

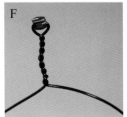

F

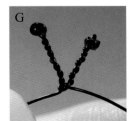

G

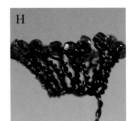

H

with one bead on the loop approximately the same height as the first. Twist this loop the same way as the first, so that the bead sits on top of the stem. If it is difficult to twist, use nylon pliers. Apply pressure gently so the bead does not break. (G)

9. Continue technique until you have twenty stamens. Leave a 3" tail at the end.

10. Twist the two tail wires together to form one stem wire. After the stamens are completed, it will look like a crown. The stem wire will be to one side of the crown. Set aside until assembly. (H)

Petals (make eight)

11. Basic 1", three rows, RTPB. After third row, cut 8" off of wire. To make scalloped edges, add enough beads so the next row will stop three beads below the top of the previous row. (I)

12. Bring wire from back to front and hook it under the third bead in the previous row. This is very similar to lacing. The wire will come through to the front, in between two beads. Add enough beads to go back down the same side of the petal. Keep the bottom of the petal pointed. Make one scallop on the other side by adding enough beads to stop at the third bead from the top of the previous row.

13. Bring the wire from the back to the front and hook it under the third bead in the previous row. (J)

14. Finish the scallop on this side by adding enough beads to complete the last row. Keep the bottom pointed. Trim so one long wire extends. (K)

Calyx (make one)

15. Make eight continuous 1" loops, leaving ⅛" between each loop. Leave a 3" tail at the beginning and end. (L)

Leaves

16. Cut a 10" piece of 30-gauge wire. Place one bead on the wire. Make the two ends even and cross the wires approximately 1" from the end. Twist the two wires from the point where they cross to the end of the wires. Make the twists as tight and smooth as possible.

17. Trim any excess wire that did not get twisted. The twists must go exactly to the end of the wire. Press the wires of the loop together so that the bead falls to the end. Make a small curve in the wire so that you can use your bead spinner to add beads to the wire. (M)

18. Make four stems with 2" of beads. Make four stems with 1½" of beads. Make four stems with 1" of beads. When you have the correct number of inches of beads on the wire, turn the stem upside down so the beads will be at the bottom. Push the beads down so there is no wire showing. (N)

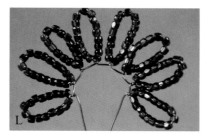

19. Untwist the ends of the wire. Tie ends into a knot so it is snug against the beads. Press wires together. (O)

20. Make leaf clusters by twisting stem wires together just beneath beads:
Make two: one 2" leaf, one 1½" leaf, one 1" leaf
Make two: one 2" leaf, one 1½" leaf
Make two: One 1" leaf (P)

Assembly

21. Using floral tape, cover the 18-gauge stem wire. Cut to desired length. Insert the cluster of loops for the center into the crown of stamens. Twist the two stem wires together to form one stem wire. Do not worry that the stem wire is not centered. (Q)

P

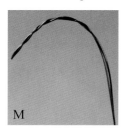

M

N

O

Q

22. Attach the center to the stem wire with 28-gauge assembly wire. Keep the wire at the top, just beneath the crown. Do not worry that the crown is not centered. (R)

23. Attach the petals, one at a time, with the assembly wire. Place the petals face up. Wrap the wire tightly beneath the beads. Add the next petal and wrap the wire tightly. Continue until all eight petals have been added.

24. When all eight petals have been added, wrap assembly wire around stem ¼" below petals. Cut wire from the spool. (S)

25. Secure the wire with floral tape. Trim the excess petal wires. Stagger the lengths of the wire when cutting. Tape stem with floral tape to cover the wires.

26. Wrap the continuous loops of the calyx around the stem. Press the loops up against the bottom of the petals. Twist the two end wires together tightly to secure. (T)

27. Press the stem wire from the calyx against the stem of the flower. Tape over the wire. Continue taping to half the length of the stem. Gently curve the flower head so that it is not sticking straight up.

R

S

T

28. Using floral tape, attach leaf clusters to the main stem. Attach them so beads protrude directly out of the flower stem and no leaf wire shows. (U)

29. Place leaves randomly around the stem, at various intervals down the stem. (V)

About the Author

Susan Ure was born in the state of Washington, but has spent the last 30 years as a resident of Salt Lake City, Utah. Her formal training was as a counselor in drug and alcohol rehabilitation.

As a young girl, Susan's interests were in rearranging her home. Her family members would return from work to find the dining room in the living room, and Susan moving all that was moveable from one place to another. Her overall talent for decorating—and more specifically in selecting the perfect piece for many store and window displays has inspired family, friends, and customers most of her adult life.

Along with a number of talents, Susan enjoys working with her hands and has shared some of her favorite beading projects with you in this volume. Especially those you can do on the go.

CONTRIBUTING DESIGNERS
Special thanks to the talented designers who shared their beautiful projects.

Doris Coghill
Donna DeAngelis Dickt
Kim Edwards
Linda Gettings
Mary Lowe
Denise Perreault
Ester Ure

CONVERSION CHART

Inches	MM	CM	Inches	CM
⅛	3	0.3	9	22.9
¼	6	0.6	10	25.4
½	13	1.3	12	30.5
⅝	16	1.6	13	33.0
¾	19	1.9	14	35.6
⅞	22	2.2	15	38.1
1	25	2.5	16	40.6
1¼	32	3.2	17	43.2
1½	38	3.8	18	45.7
1¾	44	4.4	19	48.3
2	51	5.1	20	50.8
2½	64	6.4	21	53.3
3	76	7.6	22	55.9
3½	89	8.9	23	58.4
4	102	10.2	24	61.0
4½	114	11.4	25	63.5
5	127	12.7	26	66.0
6	152	15.2	27	68.6
7	178	17.8	28	71.1
8	203	20.3	29	73.7

INDEX